Of Course

Of Course

POEMS BY

BRIAN J. WARK

Library of Congress Control Number: 2022902207

PAPERBACK: 978-1-957575-24-7
EBOOK: 978-1-957575-25-4

Ordering Information:

For orders and inquiries, please contact:
1-888-404-1388
www.goldtouchpress.com
book.orders@goldtouchpress.com

Printed in the United States of America

Contents

Dedication to the Spirit of Truth

I do not wish to be presumptuous. I am just the beneficiary, not in any way form-ally connected to The Foundation of Inner Peace and the Foundation for A Course In Miracles. However, I do want to honor eight people who in my mind principally brought A Course In Miracles into outward expression, to the point where it is now available to me and you and 93 percent of the world population in twenty three different translations, three million copies in people's hands and hearts to date.

Dr. Helen Schucman,
Robert Skutch
Dr. William Thetford
Gloria Wapnick
Dr. Kenneth Wapnick
Judith Skutch Whitson
Dr.William W. Whitson

Foundation for A Course in Miracles: https://www.facim.org
Foundation for Inner Peace: http://www.acim.org

Quotes about "Of Course"

"Laughter from his quick wit and turn of phrase reminded me that it was all a dream from which I still had not awakened. I could quote my favorite gems from his marvelous eye- and mind- opening insights. Now that I have made brief summaries of each poem, I will return to them like old friends, all waiting to comfort and amuse me again and again."

Dr. William W. Whitson, Graduate Fletcher School of Law and Diplomacy,   Former Chief Foreign Affairs/National Defense of Library of Congress

"Brian's poems touched me deeply to my core. With thought-provoking candidness, he uses personal life examples, sharing his process of moving through life's joys, pains, and matters of the heart that matter to us all. This book of poetry has the ability to invoke deep emotion as well as inquiry into the deeper nature of our spiritual beingness. It is a gift for the Soul, through one man's expression and desire to give a part of himself to us all, that we may all pick up the pieces of our lives together, and experience our wholeness."

**Cindy Lora Renard, Spiritual Counselor,
Composer and Singer, Seminar leader**

"Brian's poems reflect the guiltless nature of children of God. He shows that each and every aspect of our lives is the opportunity to learn and remember true forgiveness.

His poems are absolutely remarkable. They touched my heart in very profound way. It made me realize how many of us hover around in this illusory world while getting completely taken over by fear."

Seungnom Eugene Nam, Graduate Student – University of Toronto, Peace Presence from afar.

"Brian's love of the Course and the many references throughout the poems make clear his commitment to what it is trying to teach us. At the same time, he doesn't try to pretend that he is there. I believe his putting pen to paper through his heart as he has done can be helpful to his brothers who walk with him. I know he has helped me. PS: The pictures are priceless. They alone tell a story. Love them."

Brian Fraser, Co-Owner of the Violet Door Bookstore, Host Bowmanville ACIM Group.

"Brian Wark's work invokes an experience that elevates the reader to a place above the battleground. As I read his poetry it makes me forget I appear to be here, and takes me to a place beyond the world. I highly recommend this excellent book."

Gary Renard, the best-selling author of The Disappearance of the Universe

Introduction to "Of Course"

'Of Course' everything changed, go figure. We are no longer together as a family. This book was our swan song. Sixteen months later Alzena and Gabriela moved to Halifax accepting a brilliant academic career advancement. I remained in Ontario. Big inner curriculum!

Twenty-two years… That is how long it took between publishing my first, **Drawing Fire** and this second book of poetry. For me poems are a more intense, stripped-down essence form of communication that seeks meaning and beauty beyond the very compelling experiences of this dream. I write poems, cannot do otherwise, when life heats up. Travel, loneliness, unusual achievements, insights and breakdowns are the stuff my poems are made out of. And yes, I am a little scared to show them to you. Although I have printed out perhaps one hundred poems every year for the past ten years, between the expression and the publication, *falls the shadow*, to recycle a T.S. Elliot metaphor.

Boomers in the arrogance of their big numbers never thought they would get old, and become vulnerable, nor by some unexplained magic would our *bodies* degenerate. I am a boomer. I pretty much thought I was invincible. Younger, we never thought much of death or of dying. "If you don't like something change it." We did. Now we are looking at the unholy mess we made with our short- sighted 'me first' effectiveness. Sure there are many positive notes, but collectively Boomers are whining in their aching bones. *"Tolerance for pain may be high, but it is not without limit. Eventually everybody begins to recognize, however dimly, that there must be better way."* Karl Jung stated that after midlife at thirty-five there can be no true healing of the psyche without going to the spiritual. *A Course In Miracles* is a spiritual Thought System. The late Dr. Kenneth Wapnick, its' greatest teacher now or ever, would reply to persons sitting next to him on commercial flights by giving this succinct one sentence answer. "*A Course In Miracles* is a psychological approach to spirituality with the principal process being [sic quantum] forgiveness." If it was their time to learn and study, Ken would answer their questions. If not, that was the end of that part of the conversation, but accurate honest information had been shared.

The poems in this book are about forgiveness lessons in which there is a change of mind happening to me, usually with considerable resistance at first. That means I start out reacting with judgment, blaming and drawing from the entire repertoire of negative emotions, projecting onto the other person [or issue] my guilt, which of course I have denied and externalized. Communion is impossible alone. That is why ACIM states that relationships are still the temple of the Holy Spirit, of Forgiveness.

Early in our relationship, my wife, Gabriela made a pact with me about our purpose. With the utmost seriousness she asked me if I wanted to go on an amazing, sometimes difficult Journey with her, to return Home, to Oneness with God and All Life. She wanted a definite answer if we were to proceed. Then there is my second daughter, Alzena who is not my biological child. She was five years old the day I met her mid August 2005 when she and Gabriela came up to camp on their own across the river in the backyard acres of my restored Muskoka farmhouse. That evening we sang and told stories around the campfire well past sunset. I had said my goodnights and started up the path to my house when I heard Gabriela urgently calling me to come back. Alzena had been terribly upset and insistent. She asked point blank, "Will you be my daddy?" I gave the entirely appropriate New Age response saying we could be great friends, but 'daddy' was a very deep connection, hardly claimable after spending our first seven or eight hours together. Clearly she knew more than I did. The triangle of us has been consciously purpose driven in one direction Home from the start. There is something in the three that is discernible to other people. A good many of the poems here refer to this dynamic of the three of us.

There are over eighty black and white photos, all taken and selected by Gabriela. The idea of their inclusion was hers. Two years ago I balked, but now is the time. They in-form at another visual, symbolic level. These photos are not all posed and best angle forward. Candid, they couple with the poems to take you into our life, my life. Don't be fooled by our vulnerability, the judge- mental-ness [mostly mine], and sometimes shaky-grasp and application of *Course* principles. We are ordinary people having ordinary lessons, but we know we are going Home sooner rather than later. That is not in question.

Please understand all are not great poems herein, with respect to lyricism and literary structure. All of the poems have something to say, some considerably better than others. I hope they will speak to you in ways that resonate with you.

Even famous poets like Leonard Cohen, Lord Byron, Alan Ginsberg, or Irving Layton published in every poetry book many selections that were 'schlock', ponderous, often unpretty; poets have to write these stinkers as well to get to the gems, the ones that count and offer some enduring wisdom and beauty. Even if you try ploughing through Shakespeare's one hundred and twenty-three sonnets, you'll encounter some 'dozers', but so worth it to find the ones that particularly and brilliantly open and extend your heart of understanding in this instant of time.

Forgiveness lessons can arrive as everything from special relationship with daughter and wife, to falling off the success ladder, getting my old parked Lexus towed away, the 'halo effect', the professor of too much truth telling, ageing raging, advertising the wrong plan for salvation, past lives popcorn, mistaking freeway rumble for music of the spheres, sure-fire stock options expiring at zero, doors of opportunity that will not open, and more. Dive in, you'll find much in these poems that is accessible that you can immediately generalize to your own life. Our problems are simply past lessons unlearnt presented once again, same content showing up in different forms in front of our face as people, issues and situations. Dr. Kenneth Wapnick once said, " a good Course student is a bad Course student who forgives themself." That is the theme that carries through this book of poems.

Of Course

[this poor poem is offered apologetically in the spirit of repetition, repetition being an oft-reiterated theme of the Course.]

This book is… "Of Course"
A Course In Miracles,

Of Course, this is only one man's approximate
application of being a "garden variety" student of Course

Of course, there are many mis-taken assumptions,
I'm often off course, off Course as well

But you, you can be-cause
not effect knowing
"Perception is a mirror not a fact"
And as you well know words are
but symbols of symbols
twice removed from what is real, so

Of course, you will find "of courses" sprinkled
like punfood seeds throughout the poems*

Of course, this book is just the first course
more to come, this is your advance warning.

Of course, the eternal Lighthouse
that is Ken Wapnick's teaching
will always correct us back on course
and of course there is miraculously
Gary and Cindy.

Copyright Gabriela Ilie

Pathology of Aggregates

It wants to work, it seems to work
It seems like the right answer
for a natural projectionist. i.e.
If I can't do it myself, *this*
back-to-God enlightenment thing
then maybe I could work it out
playing in a group, a family,
a company, a club, some tribe
with a shared vision for me
surely the Group Consciousness
will plug into God's **whole is greater**
than the sum of the parts
Synergy Awards Night
and I will slip into Heaven on team Gold.
I'm talking here, like Peace man,
the great goal of Heaven on Earth
Paradiso, back to Eden
return to the Garden, Perfection
No freezing snow, perpetual
Mid-Summer's Night, sweet ripe fruit
hanging form every limb
the great Ashram in the Skye
Lion lies down with the Lamb
Cloud Blisso, Nirvana with friends…

But they have never worked- none of these confections-
because they are woven into the Illusion
and the illusion is hard wired, programmed
for breakdown, for melt-down
emotional China Syndrome,
core reactor gone haywire
Psycho Planet on steroids.

Copyright Gabriela Ilie

A Ticket to Tow [the line]

Ken's the Shepard, the Buddha
Of Business
And so Lord Lexus
Was towed a learning distance of
One hundred and thirty six dollars
Ah sure, I was setting myself up
To walk it as a victim distance
And indeed surly did start out that way
Furious at the lawmaking rich
Who move into neighbourhood
after naybourhood
by-lawing the available parking spaces
into their permit only corral,
Bring on the towers-awayers…
But stop in the name of love
Before you rape my heart…
Nobody did nothing to me Baby,
I set this up myself: and I asked
Holy spirit
Show me the truth
"Wake up and pay attention
to the safety in your driving
Are you fully present?
"I don't think so"
I had become careless, speed reckless
Depending on pure Lexus
acceleration rocketing
To jump the wait line
What exactly is my big rush?

How many buffalo do I think
I have to drag back to the cave?
Before the road rage set sin
Riding on a background count this afternoon
Lost in Stoney Creek endless stop lights
On suburban parkways, where the hell is the 403?
My nameless terror of wasting time
My precious ego's time
wasted on wrong directions.
Yes Folks this symbolically is a Big one
As I walk to dinner at Pearl Court Restaurant
On Dundas off Broadview
Talking in my cells to Holy Spirit
when I can keep the channel open.

Copyright Gabriela Ilie

Butterflies to Mexico

Perspective, well a universe in
maybe ten inches square
look up from that green green leaf
so delicious
such a total experience
absorbs you completely
doesn't it
ms/mr monarch larvae
eating
is such fun
would you know
that later
you'll be gorgeous
Monarch Butterfly
And wing your way
past palpitating panoramas
that stretch for leagues
color Palette of autumn leaves
Blue Gulfs vast
Teeming with shrimp and porpoise
Flutter past swamp trees
As broad as townships
All the way to Mexico?
Would you know?

Would one iota
Of this journey prior show?
And would you know
Dear pilgrim
The Grandness of your design?
the inner voyage
of your Awareness back unheeded
to God you never left
on wings you never needed.
October 1, 2005

Copyright Gabriela Ilie

I am having a hard time moving these poems around in cyber space. I am tired. It is after one am and I have been researching the world's largest uranium mine in Australia. Two days I have just let this poem piddle around in a rough copy. It was Wednesday morning on the Trans-Canada hiking trail to Cheltenham. It was grey, gray and foggy. The wet was in the crows' caws, in the darkness green of the far off pines. A seed of two lines only. There was more but it had left me.

November 29th 2006

Mists

The mists have settled on me
and I have settled on the
mists I have missed you so much
so much has missed me
"You miss me
when I am gone
don't you mommy?
yes darling, of course
I miss you
and my eyes mist
thinking of you
and the sadness of missing you
which [let me use it again], of course,
is missing the point
focusing on the effect
and being affected
burning the cheap toxic flame
of negative fear-based emotion
missing the body in time and space
rather than being
the cause with the mind
that shall be mine,

Miracle Mindness
Darling we are joined
forever in our
minds
i am missing nothing, no thing
you understand; I am speaking
to the You that is Me
How could I miss you?
How could I settle into the mists?
And think I could live here
Happily Everafter?
How?

Copyright Gabriela Ilie

Heart Dieting

I have been unavailable for some time-
A way of life actually.
My heart was relationship dieting,
My heart now so slender
My heart thin as a razor
So skinny really
So f—ing
separate
Actually.

Copyright Gabriela Ilie

Squacking

Squack, squack, squacking
I hear my ego squacking
It's not a nice sound
Not fun to be around

An ego that shall never
Know God
Never know love,
sees a world
of attack thoughts;
always needs some special
separate, expensive space
to project its guilt
on any and all
of the human race.

Squack! Squack! Squacking
Is that just simple irritation
disturbing my peace?
"There is no order of difficulty…"
Go ahead
Turn the page
Find the savage shock
Of scalding rage.
Squack Squack,
Squacking!!!

Copyright Gabriela Ilie

This is a paraphrased version of a conversation between a friend Michael and I at a tavern after a gym workout, one of the last we had.

Transcendentalist

You are a transcendentalist
Admit it
You are smarter than me Igetstuck
You sail through with awareness-
Dry powder- to the other side
Of the learning river
Without getting soaked
In the 'crossing'.

"Perhaps you don't
Take it personally"
is what he said to me.

Many years later, I sigh
"If you only knew."

Copyright Gabriela Ilie

The Ladder of my Success Against what Wall?

In the valley of natural movement
where I was not.
I was in some rags to riches
kindness to bitches duality
analyzing and comparing
caressing and tearing
thinking I was going somewhere
climbing up the ladder of my success
against what wall
I did not know
other than
that it was there
and you know-
standing there
in my silicon hair
I did not care…

I did not care because
all the others were there
believing that God made
this pathetic, insane world and universe
of buying and selling
and paying
and paying
the big hidden price
for this seemingly,
endless suffering, this separation curse
yet we keep longing
after some idealized expression

we romance our Arthurian legends
we moon after the Sun King and Queen:
in our heart of hearts
we all know that somewhere
somehow that true love
is the return ticket, but

We are all so quick
to turn our back on it
to shut out the God within
cycle after cycle we will not
see our mate as God:-
not good enough, not bad enough
not rich enough, not bright enough
and it's we who make it tough
because we're the Prince and Princess
don't we deserve the best?
May we please see them all undressed?
Ah, but do we have to settle for the One?
We cry pathetically
as if we lost something.

And there you have it another rung
of my sorry-ass ladder of success
up against some distraction wall
I never even considered
whether I really wanted over
or maybe unconsciously
more wanted
to just fall.

Copyright Gabriela Ilie

Cracked up to be

When the fear comes in like fog
In to settle on a whole region of the heart
It comes in and calls itself normal
that's what the ego likes
because then the fear
is treated as if it wasn't there,
invisible, not at all accounted

Even though the natural love process
of the Sons and Daughters of God
be shut down
Even though true communication
With loved ones comes
more and more scarce
until barely there
It is perfect
we are still working
toward God, our pain can be our prayer
and finally we create
the crack-up, the bust-up
the Suv smashed against the wall
spouse divorced, business bankrupt, daughter on heroin
stocks to zero, prostate cancer raging, friend betraying…
some awful attack on us,

"Why Me O God?"
that which lets the light in
Because everything a person does
From alpha to omega
Is to maximize the illumination, and
Whatever it takes
at our level of awareness
to awaken us
Will be drawn forth, perfectly
when we cry out of our misery and say
"There must be a better way."

The hologram answers…

**"And everything that seems
to happen to me, I ask for
and receive as I have asked."**1
1November 14th, 2006

Copyright Gabriela Ilie

Core Spirit Casting Agency

Moishe I see you've brought your list
of what you want to appear in, but
other than the magic stuff in Egypt
have you done any dramatic performance?
You're saying you've not been happy
with your roles Moishe?
Unfortunately we have
a very strong belief
that we need something
to be happy about
we want something
or somebody external
to make us happy:
we are not much aware of joy Moishe
so we are always running out
of scripted happy fixes
and besides, they start to wear thin, eh?
Now take Adam and Eve,
how can we get a hold
of these two anyway?
I don't have their cell number
but their DNA is ap-parently
on file with me, and yes Siddartha
I'll be with you in a moment!
Have a seat under that big tree
over there. I know,
I know you're unlimited,
I never said you weren't…

Judas, Judas, Judas
never satisfied are you?
thirty pieces of silver man
that's above Union; I tell you
it's our top price for
a second rate carpenter.
Alright, I'll give you five extra
if he makes his own cross.
Paul we're going to need you
to do a Helen Keller
road to Damascus thing
Big time method acting Paul,
we'll bring in
Stanislavski to work with you,
got to really alter that Jesus code
before it turns viral…
February 17, 2006

Copyright Gabriela Ilie

House for 'Going Home'

No,
we are not
asking Holy Spirit
for the perfect clean little
exquisite house with waterfall and
rainbox tulips, cedar loft and…
It may look like we are
but we are not asking
Spirit to enter the dream
as enlightened action
and improve the illusion,
make it better;
no, we are asking Holy Spirit
for the experience of seeing
ourselves and each other as God
by living together
in a miracle minded direction
the House is only a symbol
of that outpicturing, but
we are not attached
to nails and planks
it is for the perfect experience
in advance we give thanks.

The ego advises
that you are not the Dreamer,
but you as Body
are the Hero of the Dream
Batman, Robin and Clark Kent
all lend their muscle to the scheme
to focus on Effects-
the lazy easy focus that wrecks
awareness of the Cause
from whence spring
the very few and potent Laws
of Forever Forgiveness:-
forgiveness our only reason for seeming
to be here. You are not
the Hero of the Dream
in truth you are the Dreamer,
the Mind, First Cause, just
Be Still, Be-Cause.

Copyright Gabriela Ilie

Halo, The Effect

The halo effect states that
We are inclined to overstate, overestimate
The quality of thought and deed, words
Of someone we admire as a spiritual
Or philosophical mentor in areas
Of their behaviour that have nothing
to do with their wisdom expression
We expect them to be perfect in everything they do
According to our ego's ideal. We are set up
Big time for violation of expectation; we are set up for disappointment.
I am tired as I write this. The weight, the gravity pulls mightily.
With the light airy brightness of Gabriela
I come to expect her to always touch down
On the upbeat, the more optimistic aspecting.
When she is carrying a lot of baggage of the past
She can bump along bottom real good; she can
Pull out the daggers and never register the slashes.
Her Grumpiness at first, almost doesn't register
This can't be, this is not my Gabriela
This is not how she shows up in my mind, yet
She says caca, real intense, with a pundit's
sophistry and street person's capacity for direct
dirty hits, voice tones of the Arctic professor
"I'm going to hurt you a lot,
Don't screw with me" is the subscript
Maybe we better wait this one out
Until we are face to face.

And I can handle this for some time units
Until I run out of "this is a cry for love coupons"
You see, I am counting, keeping track
Looking for the straw that will
break the camel's back
and that, that dear friends
is pure and simple reaction…

I didn't finish it, couldn't finish it
just now or then
let's just leave it at acknowledgment,
then on to 'show me the truth Holy Spirit'
leave it up to Him.
Another case of I truly
don't know what to do.
As it turned out this was my set-up
for "the no-mater-what" forgiveness training program
that repeatedly and demonstrably
exceeds ego's capacities
causing intense frustration and surrender, ha!

Copyright Gabriela Ilie

RC Crossed Legs

The RC Church,
very heavily into pain,
is really an interpretive artist
putting a wood cross between Jesus'
legs rather than see the soul embrace of
his lovely sainted wife and equal co-teacher,
Mary Magdalena, happily occupy that space.
If Spirit is about the body
we should really obsess and confess
about the immaculate conception,
and religiously we mostly do;
If spirit is not about the body
the body is nothing-
as is the world nothing-
And we don't care a snot snuff
about all this illusionary
birth hoopla stuff
that makes your Christmas
matter mightily
for about half a billion merchants.
November 10, 2005

Copyright Gabriela Ilie

The four f alliteration poem

I read about the ego, of course
Ken Wapnick is my preferred hemlock
to kill off the ego
I drink it down cheering
nodding excitedly about the truth:
later, not much later,
the denial valve flutters open
and the foolish fluid of forgettery floods,
floods soothingly eradicating resolve,
excepting, at the tiny mad idea
still firmly remembers not to laugh
as if this was duty good to do,
as if this is the real spirit
good to chew.
January 20th, 2012

Copyright Gabriela Ilie

Meta-for?

Verily
Thou has spoken
I am broken
Like a wheel
lifted off its hub
disconnected from the revolution
that made my mileage
my record, my authenticity
where I met the pavement
in my journey travelled:

God where is my new meta?
Is my new meta held up somewhere?
Somewhere on the back tracks?
What is there to improve?
What solution can I become
Part of?
Who and what
can I fix?
How can I get up
to my old tricks?

The old illusion distractors
the boredom harvest tractors
that pull that stinky load of separation-
that crusty *manure of thought,*
pure organic condemnation.

Or I could just sincerely ask,
"What is it for?
and that would be
my new **meta-for.**

Copyright Gabriela Ilie

Jellybeans tightfisted in the jar

I am waiting for myself
in the clearing
I am seeing
how much I conditioned myself
on the great Mammon measure
of time and money
how much I had put in
and how much I had expected to get out
and could not let go
of the jelly beans
tightfisted in the jar
until I got my 'due' [do]
even though
it meant my capture
and I never saw how much
I was like Ebenezer Scrooge
and like everyone who
colludes continuously
with ego to keep our Whirled going.

Copyright Gabriela Ilie

The Prof Who Would Not Stop

Thursdays lecture UTSC CROSS-CULTURAL PSYCHOLOGY, a
student cries out in the Lecture Hall

M'am can you please
give me a break?
Can you stop now?
You have given me so much
to think about.
MY BRAIN HURTS
Please, I need to stop
go home now and
really think about it.

I need to talk with my fiance
about stripping down to the core,
and see if we truly want
to go forward: if there is
only essence, only truth
to have from each other.
Or are we just jerking around
in a tired dance
against lonely?

Copyright Gabriela Ilie

Gravestone to mark the Scream

I was out
stumbling around
in the stone quarry
of the Future
hunting for my gravestone,
my century marker
lest they forgot I was here,
here nowhere,
pretending
to be somebody,
doing something
somewhere:

It's okay mate
don't worry 'bout me
it's nothing really,
just a bad dream-
and like this very indulgent now-
sometimes a very sad **Scream;**
that's why Edvard Munch's sold
for a hundred and twenty million hollers
at the Earth Auction
where you can buy anything
And yes people will always pay
damned good money for misery.

Copyright Gabriela Ilie

Future Garden

You will lose down to your last penny
all your money gone puppy…
live- we will live in a little
secluded, nature enveloped home
with stunningly sparse furnishings
no tv, no radio
we walk and rest in simple gray robes
sufficient financial energy will come through
Gabriela's university teaching job
hard won and kept
but essential to provide for externals
in the world of form

And surprise, big surprise wrt Commodities
it has been so, *"you will lose and keep on losing a lot of money"*
witness the terrible fill on heating oil,
half of what the day of sale expected
go to the end of the line puppy
and chew on the slipper of hard done by-
And silver, your old friend, looking
to get out since January 25th
and not being able to,
going instead to the cold
hard arms of Zero.

Copyright Gabriela Ilie

Shared Vision

I was there, lawn devas
and cartwheels in the sun
sweet sleep and afternoon talks
with Deo in the Sanctuary
And Findhorn
told the world
that a shared vision
birthed beautifully
from group consciousness
and tangible unconditional love
would save the Earth
I believed that.
Believed that mind body and spirit
could get together infusion style
we could bring God Spirit
into the illusion and create a paradise
Heaven on Earth, Eden for us
even for you if you wanted
to adopt the model
of Planetary Village, City of Light,
our kind of spiritual vision export.

Our sister Community, Auroville
which art in India
cradled the teachings of Sri Aurobindo
Integral Yoga- very good deal -
rise up that hot kundalini from the base
and sexual charkas
and bring down the pure white light
through the crown and third eye
Light Spirit come into my Body
God we invite you to the illusion,
how could you refuse?
Apparently He did
Did you not hear
the news?

Copyright Gabriela Ilie

Assassinating

Even for this world
it is a little out there, insane;
I was so dislocated
I was talking in the third person
about assassinating myself:
then I really surprised myself
I found in
that I had already done it!
do you ever check your words
their composition?
how about this?
ass ass in [h]ating
when I kill you I kill myself
when I kill myself
I kill you.
Every murder is a mass murder.
Yet every mass murder just kills one, one ego dying of guilt
over and over again
in the most radical nightmare we did ever imagine
And we remembered not to laugh be cause murder is serious business
Right?

Especially when there is a God involved,
or so
the story goes
And it is my story
I have been sticking to it for eons of illusionary time
that is what a good nightmare is made of.
Trust me, but then, Why should you?

Copyright Gabriela Ilie

It Takes A Long Time To Be Indecisive

It takes a long time to be indecisive
It takes so much time
It wears a body out
Whatever happened to your talents?
Whatever happened to your looks?
Whatever happened to your High Q
your apple cider wit and cruel
specialness that got you invited?
Now, as Jeff Bridges laments in
True Grit, *"I'm getting old*
fat and ugly: I kill to get by.
It's what I know".

Of course questions are
propaganda for themselves
propaganda for the belief systems
that the questions represent and propagate and give voice to
insisting on their stand-up legs
"Listen to me,
listen to what I believe in"
and I am going to stuff
the whole damn advertisement
into this innocent little question
in which I am pretending
to make you the expert
that I am, if you only
listen closely to my question.

Anyway Take a Max And relax,
"It's going
to make you
a better listener"
That's what I need
from you.
January 7ʰ 2011

Copyright Gabriela Ilie

It Shall Come To Pass for You

Taking care of someone close
is explosive the most
when they are overwhelmed,
when they be sick,
when they feel be-trayed
by their body and by all the people
who mostly just no longer care: -
all those who somehow implied
they would be there
when the river freezes over
and the diffuse instrument
of their dis-ease is not readily available
for good effective outside
projection of denial.
They will hate you then.
You the up close one will
be hauled up to be the screen.
they will hoist you up
they will put on you
what they will…
It is just, just not the way you think you thought.
"I **am** *responsible for what I see.*
I choose the feelings I experience, and I decide upon the goal I would achieve.
And everything that seems to happen to me
I ask for, and receive as I have asked."[1]

You see the show must go on
The whole drama of the Earth spin
must be spun. The Sin Guilt and Fear
definitely must appear.
Can't stay in here for them.
You're it!!! Sister, son,
best friend, you're the one.
Yep, thrown out, extirpated,
externalized, you're cannibalized
And no matter how hard you try
to keep the blame baffles open
I repeat again, you are the Screen
and it can get pretty mean,
Is any of it fair, or true?
Do you deserve it illusional-ily?
Probably not,
No for all three questions
But does that in any way matter?
in an insane system that spins
its turbines on sin guilt and fear
when the overarching protocol
is "get that poison [I made]
out of here."
So yes, so no
you are in exactly the right place
with the right person[s]
at the right time
this is your movie
your script
you damn well wrote it
to forgive, to wake up, to illuminate

This is your Brother, your Mother
you have come in peace
walking with your Teacher
Holy Spirit
that they may come to you
to bring you Home,
"I will be healed
when I allow Him
to teach me to heal."[2]
ACIM forever.

Copyright Gabriela Ilie

Above The Battleground

*Acknowledgment: this is Gabriela's
kernel idea.*

Most men and women
have not a clue
about what is needed
to sustain a marriage.
Marriage is Comradeship.
Like in war. At first
It is glamorous and romantic
lush colours, parades and exquisite tailoring
But soon it is bound
to turn painful and dangerous.
This One or the Other business
will pound the hell
out of the relationship
and sure as Caca
the compromise deal of
mutual sacrifice will
cave in at some surprising point…

"You, you do not look like
my best interests any longer
So long Pal!"
Marriage and life here
in the dream is a battlefield
A marriage of true minds
must needs rise
above the battleground
and operate there
in truth, beauty and love
with Holy Spirit as Teacher
forgiving what one sees
and seeing to forgive.

All relationships exist
solely to afford opportunities
for Forgiveness.
Marry, and believe it!

Copyright Gabriela Ilie

Speak To Me

Speak to me
in ways I understand
Kindness will work
will you come take my hand?
Speak to me in ways I understand
that touch deeply my heart
and flush my cheek
that ends this romantic notion of soul
and makes me weep
Give me a mission
noble and clearly defined
something richly appointed
doth outwardly reward
and uplift my mind.

And Speak to me of humor
I am early on the Path
full of serious specialness
at which I need learn to laugh.
Lord hold me in Arms of Beauty
for I am stuck against ugly and fat
And I would not Know
That it is I that is that.
O Speak to me in ways
that I understand
man to woman and
woman to man.

Speak as one who
would understand,
Speak as One.
Who would understand?
January 29th 2011

Copyright Gabriela Ilie

Remember to forget, Remember to remember

Perhaps Selective Memory
is a key to enlightenment:-
We must remember to forget
Forget the judgment,
Forget all about a person
that is not sweet kindness,
Forget all that is not beauty,
all that is not loving and goodness:

And we must remember to remember
All that brings us present
to the eternal now
with peace and
joy in our heart.
February 12, 2011

Copyright Gabriela Ilie

Paying Attention

Paying attention to the ill-u-sion
makes more separated fragments appear
there is always something more
appears when we pay attention
another surprise galaxy,
ten thousand new planets
in supposed empty space;
or another famous pilgrim disappears
without leaving a trace.

When I am gone
they'll carry on
as if I never was
Brian they'll say
was here for a day
Why?
Well, I suppose
just because!
When you are dead
the great water
passes over your head
as if you were never there
And guess what my friend?
You never were,
So why, why should
you care?

Copyright Gabriela Ilie

Ken W

Everybody who is everyOne
reads your books and writings.
Truth cannot be, is not, ignored.
But it frightens the pilgrims so-
some often pretend that
they are fast asleep or bored.
And you Ken
[ken = Yes, the affirmative in Hebrew]
You express the Holy Truth
yet still can say *'those dirty bastards guys'*
with Brooklyn fervor and
without judgment when
only that applies.
When we wake up
to the wake up call
many will have woke up
be-cause of your
refusing to be small.

for February 14th Valentine's day
the heart is a symbol of the One relationship

Copyright Gabriela Ilie

Dear Gabriela

It's Valentine's Day

And I would just like to say

You Re-Mind me of the Memory
of God's Love

Pure and clean, whole-ly
out of the Dream

On the other hand
Special love is always
"on Special"

Not the bargain
we bargained for

With sacrifice,
love grown cold
love on ice
special love to special hate
and that's never very nice

But no matter what we do
no matter where we roam
our love will point us always
in the One Direction 'Home'

Peace be with us always

Love Brian

Copyright Gabriela Ilie

Your Plan For Salvation

this was brought to you by Alzena
in the form of a question

Is this your plan
for Salvation?

This anger with which
you are boiling over
Is this your plan
for Salvation?

No?

What is your plan of Salvation?
Have you given this some thought today?
Or did you just pick it up on the way
from your many and distracting sources
the loudest, flashiest, most
repetitious voices.

Yes I know we can find it
from your behaviours,
But is it really your choice?

Is it what you want it to be?
Is it really a plan that'll set you free?

Copyright Gabriela Ilie

Origin of Man

Without question
I absolutely know
the origin or man.

Man definitely comes
from the Mind and
from no where else.
Pay no attention
to what scienceman sells

And guess what?
"Ideas leave not
their source"
Derivation from eternity
is a very short course.
It has never been a journey from to *to*,
or something you could force.

Copyright Gabriela Ilie

Biggest Betrayal

What seems
The biggest betrayal
is unquestionably among
the most advanced forgiveness
lessons you will face
for it needs come from so up close
one must nearly say "within"
so great the shock to self esteem
you'd swear our face doth wear
our most dark and guilty sin.
Forget about some surface loss,
some maybe pain of secret yearning
The biggest betrayal
will completely take you in
So all of your Heavens
will seem burning.

Our personal lengthy narrative about the film…

Copyright Gabriela Ilie

"The Adjustment Bureau"

They say "listen up"
when they anticipate that irritation
will be a useful tonic to attention.
So listen up Butter-Cup
while I tell how my wife Gabriela and I
\adjusted to the movie
The Adjustment Bureau
which we had never heard of
let alone intended to view
all the way through
with our mouths wide open.
We lovingly delivered our daughter
Alzena to her biweekly visit with
her biological father- pickup point
Yorkdale shopping Mall off Hwy 401.
That was six o'clock and the movie that
we had Toronto Star tracked
was the 2010 winner of the Academy Awards
Oscar for Best Feature Film, "King's Speech".
We had had it circled to see for some time
yet it had eluded us. Not this time! 6:50pm
2190 Yonge Street at Eglinton, Canada Square
we parked a couple of blocks away,
twenty five minutes to spare, paid for
our tickets Theatre Five on the left Sir and
bought the popcorn, were seated and eating
voraciously by 6:35, all's well, but where

are the previews, the trailers of
emotional glamour to get the drama juices
flowing. It seemed to start a little late.
That was a clue, visible as tip-off
only to you, we were too well settled in …
Big lights and jazzy music
TONIGHT'S FEATURE PRESENTATION
And it started without us,
We went right into American city
Senate race pre-election scenes,
Matt Damon looking healthy wealthy
approachable and the people's choice
making a promise speech, bright teeth smile
in a damn fine voice with witty rejoinders,
but aren't we missing something?
Where's the King?
Is this some strange flash forward,
some American grand nephew somehow tied
in magically with The Simpsons, family of the
abdicated King's divorcee American wife?
My how we trust the filmmakers
to splice it all together!
Then the first climax comes:-
Damon's character stumbles on
nasty old compromising photos conveniently
released to press when he is six points ahead
just days to go, Whoops, the candidate's dead.

Yeah I know but where's King George?
He's nowhere Man. Instead, in an instant
there is an alternate time/space insertion
spliced worlds, parallel realities interacting
Spiffy determined men in ominous little dress hats
passing at will
in and out of our world, a puppet stage,
and they got the strings to do all manner of things
to us, baby to us. They were manipulating
Damon's character [let's call him Jack].
They knew much more than him
and he was an unwilling puppet- he didn't get off
on not being cause, just an effect. They were
pushing away the effects of a variant ripple
that could take Damon right off course
away from their plan for him to be
a revolutionary benevolent President
of the United States of America.
A brilliantly attractive woman he met
by chance in the men's washroom catalyzed
an immensely appealing, unpremeditated concede-
defeat-speech that was going to catapult him
into the next ascendant stage of his political destiny.
But very essential that woman exit, because of
pasts deeply entwining, otherwise
neither Jack nor she with her future fame
as a seminal dancer/choreographer
would fulfill their critically significant scripts.
And this ultra reality group reporting to the *Chairman*
would have their higher level of awareness plans
rudely crashed with tragic consequences for the Human Race.

Now that *Honest Speech* of Jack
with the right degree of spin scuffed shoes
telling the truth to the people would propel
him *direction* White House and invisible Hierarchy
inspired leadership that would steer the planet
away from its determined "**free choice**"
path of annihilation through violence and desecration.
Oh the **Adjustment Bureau** representatives/agents
didn't shy away from detailing our Earth tragedy explicitly…
Jack, smart-assedly notes that
"Things aren't that great for us now."
Bureau man replies, "Yeah but you [sic, *at least*] **are** still here."
clearly implying that without their continuous
higher level intervention we would
have blown ourselves away and would no longer BE.
We were fifteen minutes in:
Well we knew we were in the wrong theatre
Yep, both were about speeches, mind you
But we were locked in our seats, stunned
with the ironic applicability of this theme
historically to both of our lives.
EARLY, almost fantastical magical achievements
in the Playhouse of the Illusion for both of us;
accustomed to success and praise; then staggeringly
painful reversals, blockages, stubborn unsuccessing,
yet inner knowing of mission path despite outer
friction and *'don't touch'* policy away from
even simple normal ego rewards.

We came away feeling that we had been
cross intervened, [*however that metaphor
gets worked out]*, to receive a message
timely to help each of us go through
experiencing substantial, in the illusion distress-
money paucity and strong contra-indication
academically for Gabriela, shipwrecking
Salesmanship for me. What we have created here
is a failure to be important and cherished,
respected, in the games we are used to winning
and winning handsomely.
Yes it was a movie-communicated symbol
but it induced a re-examination of
[1] the seeming outward contrast
of our individual experiences
[2] the seeming contrast of success
[4] and achievement quantumly
with the long seasoning on the cold wet rocks of failure, betrayal,
insult, slander and disrespect. In other words,
The re-assertion of the ubiquitous 'Caca Factor'
harsh operative that guarantees
this composting that renews the cycle
of drama and distraction that seem
to keep us here endlessly charged with
the negativity of sin guilt and fear.
What a birthright!

The movie is about breaking through,
accepting possibility from the apparent impossible.
It is about the Lie of Levels
It is about More Advanced, Higher Being, Aliens
who may direct the salvation of our planet
and species from behind the scenes [seens].
But they ain't Holy Spirit, they could never know the
whole story, all of the motives, hence the tangible spectre
of manipulation; the uncompromising premise
of Separation, of insidious inequality
Sin, Guilt and Fear by which
the solving of one problem
makes a myriad of other problems
springing hydra snake headed
because ideas leave not their source.
How could it be otherwise?
We can't bring the light to the Illusion,
We needs bring the illusion to the light.
You guessed it.
Quantum Forgiveness is the way,
the Truth and the Light,
the reflection in the world
of God's Perfect Love.
April 2011

Copyright Gabriela Ilie

The Loss

From golden yellow
in just a day
elderly dandylions
blowing hairy kisses
in their skinny gray underwear
yes gone to seed
looking much less dandy
no longer decked out
like the sun's eye candy
then there's Stevie Nicks 2011
sorry folks, I have no voice
but I have to sing
I have no choice.
We lose it all
our hair, our teeth
and all the animal life force
underneath
We lose our fame,
our achievements and our name
we've lost all that before
we even start this game
ideas leave not their source
Loss of power
loss of force

Our Father which art in Heaven
Who dethroned you?
Was it me?
Did I think a murder weapon
could ever set me free?
"If it's one or the other,
why not, says ego,
let it be me?"
May 22nd 2011

Copyright Gabriela Ilie

May Beth

Alzena
leaning on the fence
of another life,
"surely I can say anything
I want to my younger sister"
Smart alec wise-cracks,
definite ankle biter,
and whipping the poor legs of
her dismayed mother,
who says,
"Why must my anger
burn white hot
before you will stop?"

Copyright Gabriela Ilie

MoreAutopoems
[first thought written perilously on steering wheel]

1. SPOKES

We are in a room together
diligently studying the Course
or possible at home alone
we seem to be getting it…
Then in a flash,
without a warning
the vessel's whirled
and we are caught in the spokes
of the too-much-with-us world.
May 18th 2012

Copyright Gabriela Ilie

2. DISAPPEAR

I'm afraid
to be without fear
afraid that without
guilt, I would disappear
and I would! Oh Dear.
That takes care of that
self-modulating
Yet I must not resist
being upset, for
If I look with spirit
I need do nothing
and nothing need be done
but what is done is done
through me.

Copyright Gabriela Ilie

3. AS IT IS

See the problem
as it is,
[Holy Spirit show
me the truth] Not the way
I set it up
to fail and
feel guilty.

Copyright Gabriela Ilie

4. HORSE

instructions to make this song

Don't confuse symbol
with source
And don't live your life
choked with remorse
and regretting the loss of
the damn good horse
that you rode in on
to sing this great song.

Copyright Gabriela Ilie

6. YOU GOT NOTHING

Bring the evil right
up close to observe, Even if it would
you un-nerve
and possibly even
seem to kill you.
You got **nothing**
to lose.

Copyright Gabriela Ilie

7. YOUR METAPHOR

Don't know how
I'm going to use this one…
the shampoo of spirituality
I'm going to have to leave it
for you to puzzle out
tho' it seems like a
good metaphor.
You're a far better
writer than me.

Copyright Gabriela Ilie

8. WANTED TO

If I feel something-
**call it anger, sadness,
shame, betrayed-**
I wanted to feel that way.
There's no accident,
no victim,
and no external blaming
is ever reclaiming
my innocence
that in truth
I never lost.

Copyright Gabriela Ilie

9. - CENTRE

In the dream
the spokes of human endeavour
the big tries at distraction salvation
may seem bright and inordinately clever
They point out away from
the peaceful centre
And the wheel goes nowhere
because it is not connected
through the centre
to anything.
Nothing is happening.
But when we let go
to Holy Spirit, to Jesus
He uses the spokes
for forgiveness, taking us inward,
into the joy and peacefulness
of the centre.

Copyright Gabriela Ilie

10. - SWEET AND GOOD

I have an ego.
My ego has me
and mostly does
the talking.
I'm trying to get over
Wrong Mind with
its sick neuroses
by developing a Right Mind
that doesn't hold grievances
that does not hesitate to
retract its projections
and truly forgive.
It could get to be
rather sweet and good
this Right Mind of mine.
But whoops, can't stay
to play, it's still me
still an identity
an "I" that is separate
and thus ego
that has to go,
Bring on
stage V of Trust-
the Dark Night of the Soul-
Surrender I must.

Copyright Gabriela Ilie

Music of the Spheres?

I went out back
looked a long time
through the tall white pines
it was so beautiful
I thought I heard
the Music of the Spheres but no, not so
it was the night traffic
of trucks and cars on the #401
So exquisite, so forever
so for a car-oil culture
to be expecting the eagle
finding the vulture.
May 22, 2011

Copyright Gabriela Ilie

Hear Earth Cracking

Though the Son of God
has nothing lacking
I can hear Earth cracking
from here
though it's happening there
Plus 6.6 on the seismic scale
Earthquakes in some part of the World
every other day:- droughts, tornadoes,
monsoons, rivers flooding. Birds
are aberrant on every continent,
the core is in movement, the electro-
magnetic fields are in some disarray,
the sun solar flares are wild-eyed,
storms of neutrinos pour through
the rip-the-tear in our
atmospheric mantle
Asteroids might collide and blast us to bits
Fish are breaking all of the rules
for shore[sure] leave
Humans are less, so
temporarily less "beings"
and more automatons frantically
pressing the bar lever for the cheese.

"Give me my cheese!!!
Where's my fucking cheese?"
only sporadically rewarded
farther and farther between,
we go spastic with speed.
Electronics push way past overdrive
goodbye natural human rhythms
we are all contract workers on Earth
with three jobs and no benefits
Globalization is manipulation,
is hospitalization for
the Baby Boomers
We betrayed ourselves
we said no one told us
the consequences, the outcomes
of technology. We did not ask,
we didn't want to know
so we didn't find
until the unedited speed
stripped our collective mind.
We split the atom, split the Earth
Heart in two, it became ten thousand
then the sick, sick trillions of Finance
swirling in the sovereign debt dance.
So sad we don't know how to quit
until we're knee-deep
in our own vomit and shit
and our starvation's eating it.

Copyright Gabriela Ilie

I am what I have taken

Something about the 4th and 5th Laws of Chaos which almost no one remembers; we strive to forget so we won't have to correct- just keep taking. And yes murder is the inevitable consequence of the ego's thought system

If you have it
and I don't
Surely you took it from me.
And I certainly don't have it
We're talking basic Scarcity here.
True you were kind to me once
I needed you
But dependence like familiarity
almost always breeds contempt
And what was special love
turns to hatred
to envy and jealousy.
I want and am entitled
to what you have of mine
that you obviously must have
taken from me
because I don't have it
I'm worked up about this
and I deserve it.
Give it to me
Or else!

Copyright Gabriela Ilie

The 'nots' disappear

When a wife becomes a sister
You became a brother
Present and past
It went both ways
on all the inner plays
of time
along the habit lines
of re-viewing over and over again
that which was done a very long time ago
and never happened.
Brother/ Sister what you think of that?
We tie the time line with
a multitude of complication knots
to keep us busy with death
And then with a flick of the mind
from mindless to mindful
the 'nots' disappear
vanishing the world and the universe
with them to never never land
nothing happened never was.
Truly 'nothing' happened
And silly we,
We thought it was
Really something.
May 6th, 2011

Copyright Gabriela Ilie

May the fifteenth Half Time

The half is here
the half is has arrived
half time as fast as if
we had time
we didn't expect it
we say we can't believe it
but the half is here:
another month has lost
the footrace to not happening
Half over, it has to be acknowledged

Has it been that many DVD's?
I have half a mind
to go back to April,
Whose Dream
is this anyway?

Copyright Gabriela Ilie

You stuff

You still want to be
a better happier you;
Part of the Happy Dream fairy tale
is to improve the dream
And at the end of Stage IV of Trust building
it's looking good
Forgiveness is ticking along just fine
Grievances are thinning out
And you're getting better at being kind
You're still you
'tho more in your Right Mind
But Thou't not you
And it's coming as advertised…
the explicit experience of losing
the goal of not to be more happy in the dream
But to Awake from the Dream
Good-bye dream
And good-bye to any identity,
Bad or good, within the dream
Stage V will eat you alive
not a highlight for the Body
Stage VI is unplanned
Not something the you that's you
would understand.

*You may or may not want to visit ACIM, third part The Teachers' Manual
p.10 The Ten characteristics of Teachers of God, under 1.Trust*

Copyright Gabriela Ilie

Hall not Hell

They say [the famous ones from the House of They], that when one door shuts, another one opens. They neglected to mention how long you might have to wait in the hall before that other door opens. And this other door may not be at all attractive to you. It may even be repulsive, perfect as it may indeed be for your spiritual growth.

Yes my mate
we are out in the hall
on attend, on attend…
our weary ear pressed to the wall.
Is this the door
that will open again to success?
Or must I wait on,
wait on fate:
A job my ego detests?
And guess what?
We're still out in the hall,
Obviously God
didn't hear me at all.
I want what I want
And I want it nowly
I want it the way I want it
Or my religion's going
to find me quite owly.

But yet the door does not open,
Some door, any door, **come on**!
Get me out of this godamned hall
If you don't let me out
I'm going to be climbing the wall.

Life in the hall, actually
is the time space of learning
undoing, forgiving
letting go of ungainly yearning.

Copyright Gabriela Ilie

Things have a life of their own

It seems half of my life
is taking things off
and putting things on,
then putting things off;
picking things up to go somewhere,
then rounding up the same things to return
with an endless corridor of things to learn

This things thing is big
I obviously need distraction
in a huge way

Sometimes, unfortunately
these kind of things are all that I've got,
And they are never enough!

Copyright Gabriela Ilie

Late Mate Observation

She's good at putting things together
threading subtle connections
she's good at *so-ing[all spellings]*
and knowing
which way the
innerwind is blowing.

Copyright Gabriela Ilie

Died

I died last week
I came back as me
that was a surprise
for tired eyes
to see
And we're not sure
which part of the dream
is dreamable
what part is dementia
and certifiable,
what's quasi reliable
or finally screamable?
January 30th 2011

Copyright Gabriela Ilie

The Dead Flowers

Someone,
someone has to throw out
the dead flowers.
The yellow roses
that meant so much
as a symbol of undying love
their clean gorgeous scent
filling the nose, sweet memory
of thoughts that were sent
dreams that were meant
to come true and keep you close.
But now the edges are brown,
the stems stoop
petals are falling on everything
and the water really does
smell like poop.
Some one has to throw out
the dead flowers
take the bodies out
flush the sewers of illusion
try not to once again
pretend away the confusion
of taking body for mind
seek for find.

Copyright Gabriela Ilie

Day Poster

I have woken
more beautiful to the day
I have asked my God
to come out to play
I have smiled at the tiny
I have laughed at the big
I have rolled in the mud
with the fool and the pig.
February 8, 2011

Copyright Gabriela Ilie

Leaning without meaning

Ezra Pound shouts out
in Pisa Italy
"Hey you there with the arsehole!"
It's silly to say
but it got my attention
I was Mussolini's military attache
preternaturally impressed
with the emphatic;
I always would say,
"If uncertainty reigns
bring on the autocratic."

Copyright Gabriela Ilie

June 21ˢᵗ 2011 this follows a conversation with Gabriela in which she outs to a surprised me, several of our friends who substantially do drugs, and patiently identifies the behaviour dysfunctions that ensue and how it handicaps true meaningful friendship.

Stoned Out Of You

I know
you think drugs are normal,
as in understandable, accepted
and pretty much a way of life,
Everybody does a drug thing, right?
It is the way it is, and we are.
Period.

But I submit. It is not so.

With Drugs
your native knowingness,
your truth experience,
the truth telling,
is **STONED OUT** of you.
You learn to smile as you hate,
learn to lie, and dissimilate
To party, to mask and worst of all
to deceive yourself and
every one closest to you.
You refuse to look
to admit light, let alone acknowledge
the dark despair you feel.
You are shrouded, clouded
the alerting pain pushed down.

Your clarity, your innocence
your natural response to
legitimate cues of fear
is **STONED OUT of you.**

And you,

You helped set this up
you agreed to this
massive limitation
of your potential.
Once started, too often
Drugs become a lifetime user plan
You are a captured market, the supply
is always available, expensive, smart
and enticing. The mystery set!
Some mystery! Raw self destruction,
the worst deal yet!

For love is not an emotion,
nor an acquired neuro-chemistry
Love is an ability, a talent
that must be nurtured and developed
It cannot be bought
It cannot be got.
With drugs started, you are
as in sexuality, de-flowered.
You can't get back your virginity
that perfect innocent chemistry.

And people don't want to hear
a sane conversation about drugs' effects
they go mute, don't want to talk about it
they don't want to think about it.
Distraction is the law,
socially mandated amnesia,
remember Anne Wilson Schaeff's
<u>When Society Becomes an Addict,</u>
and remember <u>Matrix I</u> which
hit us hard enough in the solar plexus
for us to consider that
we may be living out a controlled,
pain aversion dream with its
well-worn predictable pleasures
Mostly acceptable by most,
we are as 'battery operated cells'
units of energy production
and harvesting. And Intense stress
is apparently a good useful crop
to the dark side.

Some want out, want freedom.
It is to you I speak,
terrifying as the price is
or seems to be.
Parallelling ACIM thought system
where we learn that the last thing on Earth
I want to hear about
is my Fear and Hatred of God
and God's Love. It seems
We dethroned Him, usurped His Power
and murdered Him
in our addled ego dream mind.

The pain of that remembrance,
is too great, too corrosive
mindless and numb, we deny then project
our guilt as attack on external targets.
It is too painful to own
and acknowledge to ourselves.

Gabriela sees other's secret constitution
hears their thoughts- doesn't want to, but
hears them regardless; it is ego inconvenient
but it comes anyway. There you have it.
Others in the drugged plan, avoid the bright
revealing light that is spiritually directed.
As a Non-User, unconsciously she is a big threat
to them and they include her not.
They wanted a Pollyanner
but *they canna hav'er*.

Copyright Gabriela Ilie

You never know

I didn't know
you didn't know
that I didn't know.
That's why
I didn't
say No
although
I wanted to.

Copyright Gabriela Ilie

Travel tips

if you travel
don't take guilt trips
go walk the mall
of a foreign country
go to a waterfall
but don't take guilt trips.

Copyright Gabriela Ilie

University Of Movies

I've been studying progressively
at the University of Movies
meeting metaphysically
the undoing of unconscious guilt
[Illusionarily piled up in past lives]
through a strict course of nightly movies
five per week appears to be the nirvana set
a couple of nights off to eat out
and to entertain guests and talk out
other reel plots and characterizations
that invite me, instruct me to forgive
quantumly, hauntedly
these ghosts of projection
I put up on the screen of my awareness
to uncover what is hidden
in the dark theatre of my mind.
I inhabit a make-believe House of Movies
I pretend to want out
But I keep on buying
the tickets
to the show
thinking it's night, right?
I have nowhere else to go.
'cept the University of Movies.

Copyright Gabriela Ilie

Your Part

We all and each have to play our part
in this grand play of redemption,
this Son Ship that we row Home
unimaginably together as ONE.

Gandhi-Ji is said to have said:

"Almost everything that you do in life will be insignificant

But it is very important that you do it
Because No One else will."

Don't worry we will
work out the wrinkles.
Correction: we will
laugh out the wrinkles
and create more laughter
at the miracle corners
of transformation, the sharp
corners where the mind changes,
changes direction and
returns home.

Copyright Gabriela Ilie

Salesman's Lament

From the disappointment of April 9th 2011 on the road selling but not selling…

This is not my first salesman lament
in a life outside nearly everything,
But it seems I've spent
a half life
struggling to get out
of the things
I got in to.

The question: as always,
Where in the world went
that nova star of enthusiasm
that got me into this cement?

Copyright Gabriela Ilie

Russian throughway

What I like about the Russians
is their bold beating heart
is their brazen rampaging
through serial highly
engaged dramas.

Somehow they genetically know
that the way through
is to go through
to undergo

Rather than avoid
and go around,
not to stand stolidly
on parking lot ground
they go through, and
any throughway will do.

Copyright Gabriela Ilie

Wrong way, that's all I'm going to say

We bring the truth
on portable altars with banners
to our Illusion.
We ask God to officiate,
assume, "yes" and proceed,
God is now part of the Illusion!!!
A Religion is Born!!!
Churches, then Cathedrals raised
Collections collected
Bequests bequested
Red Cardinals marching double breasted.
And Praise the Lord for that,
And That.
That's where we're at!
We boast that we have converted
the illusion to truth,
The Secret is out
It's Mother's Milk
And we're out looking
for other Suckers to Bilk.
Now here's how you do it…

Keep it simple, Master the emphatic
Repeat, repeat,
our little minds are nomadic
Get used to cammand. Cammand
Repetition, repetition, repetition
And we'll believe anything you say
Say it over and over long enough
In our media-formed mind it will stay.
Then bring on the mysterious mystery
For it's the metaphor sandbox
where the brighter ones can play.
It will look good for while,
but it's the wrong way.
Yes you heard me right,
"It is the wrong way."

Copyright Gabriela Ilie

Passe

I watched your passing
in the constant flickering
of telephone numbers
and embossed addresses;
watched the debt
cut lines on your torso
the lonely cell
phones you kept
out of sentimentality
the fines that weren't
fine to pay anymore;
your crocheted cancer skullcap
the slow progressive
breakdown in capacity
to purchase your place in society
through accelerated consumption
of words.
I have watched
as if a mirror was placed
to my lips
to mark my breath.

Copyright Gabriela Ilie

You plant quotes in me

Stop trying to get me
to say what I didn't say.
You want to plant quotes in me
to further your own thesis
and farm some value
in the reference as if
coming from me
were some boon.
"Stop." I say,
"STOP!!! is
the elephant
in the room.

Copyright Gabriela Ilie

"I did not say."
I just read Dostoievky's Idiot

IDIOT

I Dio t
translation,
If I say
I'm God
t= I'll be crucified
[on the cross of t.]

Copyright Gabriela Ilie

Aftershave

A vetiver aftershave
went walking by
the Sun was setting
and so was I
reading the Idiot
I could not stop
this headlong train
of runaway pain
and stinking thinking thought
drama piled on drama
from the bottom to the top
and down again, up again
Prithee, Call the Emotions Cop!
But reading the Idiot as Christ
I could not stop.
Nothing to do with vetiver
except without it
I was not there.

Copyright Gabriela Ilie

Two Hours on a Park Bench

A lot of people pass by you
in two hours on a park bench:
some on the delicate verge
of interaction, but not quite,
perhaps too close to the start of night.
He gives his smile, but not his eyes,
'they think why risk, it may not be right.'
I do not encourage them further
though I know we are mind streaming
together. If we are One and joined
Why are we dreaming?
Be passers-by.
Leave the dream
to the sky.

Copyright Gabriela Ilie

Gabriela's Dream

from the unableness to sleep Friday Night July 29ᵗʰ 2011

A man, age sixty five,
He is dead,
Entitled, not lacking confidence
He came into our house,
so to speak,
to speak with you.
He has something important
He wants to say to you.
It may benefit.
May you pay attention
My Brian.

And so I did
and asked to hear
what I needed to hear.
It related to the movie
I had watched that night
William Hurt and who
his character was. He was
rigid, unable to drop his stone face
and be vulnerable in love
no matter what: he went to prison
for six years, manslaughter of an innocent man
who tried to break up his push/shove with his beautiful wife
outside a bar where she had followed him.

after she had miscarried their child
possibly from complications
of a prior abortion.
I feel the message to me
was to loosen up and unfreeze
my emotions, see the call for love
when my ego thinks it is
a deal breaker, show stopper.
Get over it, Brian
open your heart and be kind
Be gentle, honest
you won't mind

Copyright Gabriela Ilie

Four Ladies of Color

How do we say it now
politically correct without affront?
With a clear loving heart
is how…
Four black ladies on the Union
Station midnight train back to Ajax
were sitting together talking out
their troubles, animatedly,
in the convivial circle they had made.
I'm not here, I'm a white shadow
on the wall across the hall, aisle,
a isle of this moving living room.
I write, they can see that,
therefore I am safe within my role,
they are unconstrained…
"God he can't wait to go home…
Ah, the addiction, going up and down
Up and Down…
She's no good a mother,
better the girl go live with the grandma…
The man go,
ain't gonna stay with no ol' fat woman…
it's not right…
sassing me all the time, teenage daughter
going out with these older guys, they got money
they can buy what she got
until she ain't got it no more…"

No voices are raised,
it is a kind of funeral of desire
they are stirring the ashes
reluctantly confirming there are no coals
worth oxygenating, their clothes
are rich in oranges and reds,
they are going home to empty beds,
"Love, he don't know how
to express it."
Ajax, next
they got up and left,
I had one more stop
Whitby.

Copyright Gabriela Ilie

July 30th 2011 at Harbour Front

Harbour Front, used to be a panorama
for me of the Arts easily available
in rich concentration, a visit
out into the whole world of top level
dance and theatre and music
free or at a price I could afford.
SoulPepper was housed, great plays
four for eighty dollars and the big
outdoor stage by the lake
highlighted performing artists
the best representatives from every country
Flamenco, Egyptian torch singers,
Caribbean heartstoppers, French Algerian Blues
Asian ageless dancing, chirango and pan pipes
scaling the Andes, each the essence
of their culture. I was younger then
but then you knew that,
yet how can seven years
make such a difference?

I was coming from Muskoka, feeling free
to the weekend, I would swim in the
multi multi people watching with joy
our immigrant waves pouring
through me
over glasses of beer and wine, smiling,

there was time then,
no one was an outsider
there were possibilities, not everyone was
suited and paired up in some unit bundle
of exclusion, walking the
special relationship
showing off the dollars to buy
expensive dinners
and boat harbour tours and
anything going.

The international cookout tent was wild
with I-never-had-before tastes, the little
marketplace stalls teeming with genuine
bargains unattainable anyplace else
at take home
a momento of the weekend prices.
I bought a horsehair band panama hat,
white bleached cotton shirts, jewels
from the Nile, and shea body butter,
papaya cups with lime juice.
Frequently I ferried over to
the lush green of Toronto Island

I went home excited at what I had seen
and been, feeling wealthy in experience.
If I would walk a little distance
to side streets, the parking was free.
One by one they went, victims
to rich people's by-laws,
by permit only. Toronto costs
too much for me now.

In seven years everything has doubled
and my income has cut in half.
I am singing the song of the elders
disenfranchised by my own libretto
I wrote the **script**, then jumped
into the drama
but I don't want to remember **it**,
it being that I'm not just a player,
not just the hero of my dream.
I dreamed the dream,
I am the dreamer
and when my light needs
get too intense
I am the temple screamer.

What I learnt here tonight
is there is no going back
to re lay the track
of past pleasures, missions
and capital endeavours
I am not trained
to go backwards.
Move on, move away
from those before loves
those ancient hates
and nostalgic illusion fates
Move on and Brian,…
Get the move on!
and rejoice Brian
that you get
to move on.

Copyright Gabriela Ilie

[It's a joke boy it's a joke.]

We die alone

Not to need distraction
nor Saturday night action,
not the need to thicken
when a woman's breath doth quicken
to truly be at peace
when my illusion delivers the least
or at least the most
until we feel the surfeit choke
there is no winning policy
no strategy fit for
the lasting Hall of Fame
we die alone, this is not our home,…
Is everybody else always to blame?
I've been the two, ten thousand times
and it has always been the same
that trip to the heart of Darkness
"The Horror, the Horror, Oh the Horror"
'Terminate with extreme prejudice'
My oh my, what Martin Sheen's*
character has and hasn't seen!
This mission officially does not exist,
never existed and is never
to be referred to in the future.
Is this not the instruction for much
of the inconvenient truth we don't
honour in this dream life?

Thus the veil's restored
the hidden intentionally ignored
mindless we gnash our teeth
tremble with what's beneath
*Apocalypse Now, the film

Copyright Gabriela Ilie

The Pattern Reigns

The pattern reigns
You think "*I'm grown up*"
My parents are over there in the condo
In old age half thinking
they are still young
I'm here, I'm hep, man
But they're here
In me running patterns,
Total dawn to dusk energy fields
That run me back and forth
In the shadow theatre
Before the candlelight
Dazed, stunned by loaded conditioning
That kicks in unconsciously, automatically
With the old environment of 'home'
Become unconscious, insensitive, accommodating
to survive yet totally vulnerable…
Irish tears, my dad rides the train
of emotional extremes,
the rest of the ride is numbed
Ignores the in betweens.
And whose cells
Have I been dupe-
licating?

Copyright Gabriela Ilie

What Do I Want? That's the Question

The sawdust eyes scratch:
here I am
face tight and gaunt
my nose grown beet red
with allergies
and lying to myself
not doing what I want.

Mom and Son

Leather armed hockey bomber jacket and
ball cap still on at the table
the fifty something grey grizzled son
stares out the big front window
at the falling snow
he is a burger man
burger and chips, out for lunch
with mother. He drives, she pays
she slips him thirty bucks
"Here you pay, while I
go to the washroom", and she wonders
if he will ever have a steady job again.
What is he? dreamer, wanderer, trouble-maker?
she worries, her boy, never quite fit in
did he… *What was he trying to do*
with his life anyway? At least
he is good company,
and I need that now."

Copyright Gabriela Ilie

Cues

My eyes open from pause into slow motion
I am generating cues in my own environment
To remind me
That this is all impermanent
Not real, a mind projection
And guilt at my separation from God
Which is the invisible electricity
That runs and animates this
Plato shadow show
That we call the world, a-whirled
Always spinning mammon's fabric
To keep me covered
Never naked
Never still
Keep me fearful
On this wheel
Of birth and death
Of all that is unreal

I am generating cues
That I may awaken
And I have asked
That you help me
Please.

November 7th, 2006

I miss the most

I fear
I fear
I fear I miss the most
our talking until the end
finishing, completing
beyond time
to resolve, to finish the dissonance
to sit in council together
in trust
until we know together
what is
and what is not
and to find our way
onto the lap of Holy Spirit
and hear God's heartbeat
through His Voice on Earth.

November 14th, 2006

ISSAQUAH DOCK

Slender twelve year bridge

He wrote a poem
a slender twelve year bridge
between them
that she walked over
came right up,
asked to take his hand;
Then, not exactly right away,
she did ask him to stay
and would he please be
Going Home with her?
It took him awhile
to understand what
that meant
that he had manifested her
that she was God sent,
and that No
was never a possibility
with his own creation.

This is a thread that kept Gabriela and I in touch through time 14 years after we met initially. A poem I wrote back in the 70s and was a part of my first book of poetry "Drawing Fire". Gabriela, to this day recites the poem wherever we go and have to tell people about us, about who we are, what brought us together, what is our life's purpose. It is the seed of our relationship… so I had to include it.

Letting go

We traded our look out on the street
there was no street talk, no head talk
but something clean and sweet,
With our tears
dawn came softly
bare and magnificent,
though, incomplete.
She turned like smoke
and she was turning to me
to show me the way
to go clear
to go free.
I cried out loud
"How did you know
I needed to let go
to call my own bluff
to stop my own show?
to let the sun shine through
feel the mellow wind blow
Oh how did you know,
How did you know?
As I say these words
I feel myself
letting go, letting go

flowing the silver chord dance
that I did so long ago
letting go of the scorecard
that nearly totaled my soul
and my tiny world picture
with its fine tune control
letting go of what I once was
and what I could have been
letting go of the final word
and the comfort
that choked my dream.
Oh come free and easy
letting go, letting go
take me fast good Lord
or Lord take me slow
and when it's over
hold me close, but
let me go, let me go.
And I'm letting go
of the hero
that I thought I was
all the reasons why not
and the good ship "Because"
letting go of name dropping
and all that cheap reflected glory
my cross parked in the cloakroom
to make the whole world feel sorry.
Laughing, laughing, laughing
letting go, letting go
no mistaking the lesson
for the truth
with a giggle in control.

Letting go of the two headed mornings
of the wander-lust eyes
minds ignored in
conversations of thighs
and letting go of love
as a registered deed
of giving, conditional
to the thanks I receive.
Letting go of sickness
as an excuse not to face,
Of trying to solve
my thin problems
on the whole human race
letting go of beliefs
that carried no seed,
Of always taking more
so much more
than I wanted or need.
Letting go, letting go
so soft, so white
like falling snow
letting go till I'm naked
standing arms at my side
with no place to run
no pride left to hide
and letting go, letting go
shot full of the skye
Soul on the wing,
Ego on the die.

Endnotes

*   look for them, find Waldo

1   Excerpt from A Course in Miracles, 2nd Ed., Chapter 21, II. Responsibility for Sight (2), p. 448. Published by the Foundation for Inner Peace

2   Excerpt from A Course in Miracles, 2nd Ed., Chapter 2, V. The Function of the Miracle Workers (A- 18), p. 28. Published by the Foundation for Inner Peace